## PRAISE FOR *TWICE THERE W*



A new *enfant terrible* of the post-Yugoslav poe
landscape, Alen Hamza writes poems that osci
remembering, between the two gods of his soul—Bosnia and Herzegovina and America—between two languages, and between the life that passed and the life that is passing. Strong and fragile, documentary and fictional, born from personal and collective history, his poems face you with your own life and hurt and cure you with the same intensity.
**LIDIJA DIMKOVSKA**

In *Twice There Was a Country,* Alen Hamza delicately shows us what happens to the internal psyche during exile and its aftermath. There's longing, displacement, absurdity, yes; but oh there's also humor, surprise, and joy. These poems do not dwell; instead, they provide outlets through refreshing language that does not fear end-rhymes. It's these rhymes, playful misspellings, and the child-like detailed observations that best capture the absurdity of exile, the absurdity of war. Hamza acknowledges that "this age calls for chewing," and in this brilliant debut, he gives us "American-chewed words."
**JAVIER ZAMORA**

With these darkly magnetic poems, Alen Hamza locates us in a world of political upheaval, personal dislocation and emotional fracture with a stunning balance and decorum. Reading *Twice There Was a Country,* I feel like I am being guided by a gentle firm hand while bombs are exploding around us, and surely this is one of the best things poetry can do.
**DEAN YOUNG**

# Twice There Was a Country

Alen Hamza

Cleveland State University Poetry Center
Cleveland, Ohio

Printed in the United States of America
Printed on acid-free paper

ISBN: 978-1-880834-80-0

First edition

24 23 22 21 20 5 4 3 2 1

This book is published by the Cleveland State University Poetry Center,
2121 Euclid Avenue, Cleveland, Ohio 44115-2214
www.csupoetrycenter.com and is distributed by
SPD / Small Press Distribution, Inc. www.spdbooks.org.

Cover design: Amy Freels

*Twice There Was a Country* was designed and typeset by Amy Freels in Minion Pro.

A catalog record for this title is available from the Library of Congress.

for mama, tata, and Denis

*We must take the feeling of being at home into exile.*

—Simone Weil, translated by Emma Crawford

*Forgive me, distant wars, for bringing flowers home.*

—Wisława Szymborska, translated by Clare Cavanagh and Stanisław Barańczak

# CONTENTS

# LITTLE BY LITTLE

I left, at twelve, the town of poplars.
Pimples lined my forehead,
rifles kept young men awake.

A country of six became six countries
with one product: nationalism.
I crossed the border, an ingrown nail.

I left half my heart cradled
by the razor wire. *I will lull it*
said the wire, a life form

made exclusively of teeth.
And so surrealism
entered my life: no revolution,

no transcendence. Just the horror
of material things.
Little by little, I said fine to life.

Stopped feeding vitamins to pets,
accepted that not all cacti sting,
relegated wonder to the landfill.

## DOUBLE NEGATIVE

After sixteen years, my parents are returning home.

On more than one occasion, my father has said:
"There, I do not want to go. Here, I do not want to stay."

The Bosnian language permits a double negative.
English frowns upon it.
I have not told my father that his life is not possible in his adopted tongue.

Father's outbursts—I tell Mother—are caused by the impending change.
My mother doesn't buy it. She doesn't buy much anymore.
She used to buy all the groceries. Father was the chauffeur.

My brother and I will soon live together.
I am looking forward to it.
I am not looking forward to it.

The greatest impediment to happiness is imagining
other people's lives as better than our own.

Slowly, my father, my brother, and I
are becoming imagined people
to my mother.

What kinds of lives will she grant us,
on which shore?

# THE BODY

Silence has a mother in it and summer
refuses to move on.

Dear God, your breath is hot, your fingers long.
In the heat of Texas, under mistletoe,

I kiss the ghosts of home country girls.
Lips of Jelena, Koštana, Alma: how do you feel

about the lips
of your husbands?

Your molars hide the molds of keys
that breathe salvation open.

Run me green, give me directions
in the language of youth.

I am the library which cannot dream,
a decade unchecked, copulating with dust.

Future is Mother or Father.
Forgetting, remembering.

## ASHBERY IN BOSNIA

My town is five thousand souls long
I have told lies in the past
Given it fifteen, twenty at times
Never on purpose distance enlarges
There I took Ashbery who was tired
Of the poetry scene
And forests whose lungs are giving out
Coughing chicken nuggets with a side of tar
We walked up the mountain of Prenj
He took out his monocle and praised the *e*
The lone vowel in a forest of wolves
To help with pronunciation I said
*Prenj* is similar to *stenj*
Which the heavenly grammar god admits as a word
Meaning *wick* but which I
An earthly sufferer of no love
Meant as a shortcut to *stenjati*, to *moan*
He showed me his varicose veins he fingered
My future, tracing rivers of the body's making
May I sir take a swim in you
How strange to say most important words
With eyes
Silence pelted us
It descended like hail after one decides
Comprehensive coverage is for the rich
The clouds were pretty maybe a little
Slim, cynical and dark, partly absurd

Never sublime
Bosnian sun shining on trousers in clouds
Making their way amidst walnuts and pines
Toilet paper sleeping on the side of the path
Moss breeding to breathe the dark side
Reminds me of the Alps, a Swiss village
He said
Surveying the valley below
The earth falls and in the falling
Climbs to new heights
A higher constellation of puzzled interaction
In which wins neither war nor peace
My soul wants to live here
I said
But I have never been good to my soul
We were now at the peak and I apologized
For my country not speaking French
It's okay, Ashbery said, nobody's perfect
Life flows out of your country's mouth
It is beautiful and enough

# QUEERREFUGEECATHOLICMUSLIM

A man of my gender once said to me,
Let it go, and it will go away from you.
If in the end I realize I really wanted
to be a poem—so what?
Mary is lonely.
Said Tomaž about Mary.
Whiff of freesia in architecture library!
I architect into a teenager, all of seventeen.
St. Louis summer, hello.
And Bonnie!
You took my breath away with your damp blond hair.
In that moment all our future days
were contained.
Turtles in a pond. Singing frogs. The cat
you worried about because your grandmother
mixed her hair in cat's meals.
The grandmother who haunted my dreams
when I visited your Wisconsin palace.
Two bottles at the 34th Street Café, Tomaž!
And I walked out the back door looking
for the bathroom.
My love is a sprinter, a current piercing
stone, branches, moss.
You want a lick? says love to salmon.
And a lick is born.
You, Tomaž, both have and are
a love like that.

I was twelve and you fifty
when we stopped sharing the soil of a fable
called Yugoslavia.
Mary thinks more about you than me.
When we met she talked about squirrels
while smoking. When she put the cigarette out,
she talked about Mandelstam.
Mary, I too am lonely.
I love colors, and the salty part of the wrist.

## AUNTIE ORACLE

Auntie Zlata, first-grade teacher, prophesied
my later issues: "You will wallow in seas of milk
without the ability to digest lactose."
Since this was the beginning of the world,
lactose intolerance didn't exist and my parents
demanded an explanation.

Auntie Zlata: "He will deal in mystery without inhabiting it,
he will wear coats that are too tight, will be devoted
but not committed, from an early age
he will be an old man, full of pride and dismissive
of therapy." Socialist countries are honest.
My parents were upset: no mention of milk.

They installed mirrors throughout the house,
they decided to have another child.
I dreamt at night of Auntie Zlata and was forbidden
from taking daytime naps.
But we live so close to Italy! I protested.
My grandfather went white overnight.

Around this time, Daddy bought me a bikey.
I named it Mikey. Days went happy, very
happy.
Then
war.
Auntie Zlata?

A committee formed by Mother
prowled. We gathered up the stray dogs
for the sniff job. In her apartment we found
peeled potatoes and the TV tuned to snow.
A cat appeared.
On her collar a note:

"The war will last. Slovenia will be
the first to join the EU; Croatia second.
Our own Bosnia-Herzegovina will begin
negotiations the year before
the EU dissolves.
I'm glad I'm old."

## PRIMER RUFFLED BY WIND

The moon in me is

The summer

Salty waves reach up to feed
pedestrians scented with beach

More and more the outer world is enough

A world long with exit

A peeling, lizard-teeming terrace

Palm berries divorced from palm trees chat up
flip-flopped feet

A part of me belongs to a dead country

My ghost

# READING *CHARTERHOUSE OF PARMA* IN HERZEGOVINA

I pat my winter life, lost in words
that are lost in thought. The mind
is in the brain, the brain in space.

Fabrizio and Clelia are in love
and the moths are sleeping.
I have returned to appraise them.

I've been here before, birth-delivered.
Mother then a human with a brain.
My town is a ringtone on my phone,

it wakes me up, it keeps me clean.
Soldiers exist both when there is
and isn't war. Look,

the veins of war are bulging up
in those who govern. The forehead
holds the future; I interview mine

with a flashlight. But moths asleep
are not moths I can appraise,
so I walk over gravel, the foundation

of life. How does hope announce
itself? I ask Fabrizio. Must one have
windows, must one know birds?

The sounds Mother makes live far
away from harps, have made me
a lover of atonal music.

She cannot remember the war,
nor know another's coming.
She lives in a house with no glass,

yet a curtain.

# THE OLD BRIDGE IN MOSTAR

*for Fedja Buric*

Into green
the bridge
falls.

Its gray stones in the river Neretva,
rescue troops pull them out
before they reach the Adriatic.

Your bridge is fallen.
Don't lie,
I know you visit every day.

You like to say
*I'm searching for the soul*
*of my town.*

People so wicked
their souls
don't count.

*Where are your eyes?*
I ask after you return
to America.

*You forgot your eyes.*

## DEAR UNIVERSE

This is the first summer
that is spring.
No one swims.
Many times you have said,
Buy a small boat, load it with desires,
bring extra fuel, and glide off
into the Adriatic.
Today the sea is naughty.
Waves, white-tipped, are rolling.
I end up paddling back to shore.
A search for bodies yields an elegant,
muscled zero.
I would like to be blood
equipped with a high-resolution camera.
Southerly wind is raging,
branches are cracking.
I would like to weigh my brain
on the scale of decay, pluck
the gray hairs.
Goodbye Biosil, favorite silica supplement.
Goodbye vitamin preparations
for hair, skin, and nails.
Is getting old as fascinating from the inside?
I yawn at noon, I ban sprinklers
from the grass.
False starts are life.
I will shore the thirty gray chin hairs

against the elements and together
we will brave the springtime sea,
the whistling wind, the percolating
stares of the locals.

## IN A PHOTOGRAPH YOUR HANDS MELT

Make yourself warm,
you told me.
I lit a fire and waited.

And evening.
People disappear,
I thought.

The fire was out,
I was alone
in your house.

I looked through
your books, napped
on your bed.

Warmth is a master
from the sun, warmth
comes to make us nice.

You said,
Light a fire,
make yourself warm.

My mouth is a breath-
riding tongue:
Where are you?

I could live here—
much bigger and warmer
than my house.

I have a cold house.
In the winter dogs breathe
to warm it up.

I have known you for years.
You have a warm mouth.
You have an inside

made of sun.
You are reaching forward
in the photograph.

Where?

## THE AGE OF MONKEYS

1990 was known as the year of bananas.
Ante Marković, the last Yugoslav prime minister,

realized the grave terrors ahead
and provided the populace a treat,

nutritious and easy to peel. Was he aware
of the fruit's high content of magnesium

and its calming effect on the psyche?
His biography does not mention. His reign

is called the Yellow Age, though pundits
call it the Age of Monkeys.

Bananas continue to sell well
in all countries of former Yugoslavia.

## GOOD LUCK

One night I bought a policeman
a drink.

Then another and another.
It's a myth policemen don't get drunk
on duty.

I saw him teetering.
I was making sense.
He was prettier.

He asked about my destiny.
I don't believe in destiny, I said.
He locked me up for heresy.

Except he forgot to lock up.
I roamed the prison free.

***

## TWICE THERE WAS A COUNTRY

I am afraid of my voice.
I record it in the morning to scare myself at night.

In it lives a red pentagram.
In it lives a dead country.

Come together: clack, clack, clack.
Six times clack equals two eyes black.

Twice dead means resurrection is a visible thread.
I am nevertheless an atheist blessed.

Balkan miracles have inverted consequences.
Perverted are the hands of decay.

Twice there was a country.
And twice it faded away.

# KARADŽIĆ-RUINED ROMANCE

Little, I was salty.
On the beach: pebbles.
Me: an adult hater of sand.

At thirteen, at night, I:
the shape of a watermelon.
Pinker than the rose's ping,
spearheaded by tongue.

With Ivana to the church courtyard,
with Ivana into the hedge.
The priest up, his night-kissed cassock
covering jealous pubes.

Big, salty by foreign lake.
Exile courtesy of the violent-
haired poet. He now rots
the prison in the Hague.

Satellite TV and shaving cream:
good reasons to delay joy
to worms.

# COMING TO TERMS WITH PALAVER

1.

Travel is best experienced in the mind.
The most enjoyable is the before, the getting
ready, the skimming of things to be encountered.
We reject wisdom like a bitter melon
when we're young—not because we cannot
but because we do understand it.
The equanimity it pawns off on us
is in rivalry with the energies of life.
*The energies of life*—this is the moment
when we—I—cringe, but I do not erase.
Old, we latch onto wisdom, become jelly
to its butter. The stillness that awaits
is wisdom's bait, wisdom's tongue.

2.

Do not throw away the marginalia.
Relax and allow it to do its bidding.
If life, offended, thunders back
that all life is marginalia, we will know
it's an alien. What do we do with aliens?
It is hard to say since you are not here.
A middle-school teacher admonished me

never to approach experience without
the benefit of another's perspective.
A high-school teacher embraced me
and said, Embrace yourself!
I never know how many evenings lie
in wait.

3.

It is hard to pronounce the name of my childhood
abode, where I took to stone over sand.
It is easy to dismiss things that are far,
and easy to like people who are far.

4.

Constantly, while in it, wondering
Is this it?
and feeling
This is it—the peculiar business of human.
If I were a chimpanzee, I would still enjoy
the colors of the sunset, up on a branch
I would climb and watch.
*Extracting wisdom is busy work* has never been
said before. Unless, in some far-off corner,
farther than the sunset-revealing branch,
farther than the digital cloud, there lies

an index card in a wooden catalog,
a decaying matrix of carbon and fiber,
which remains in circulation.

## THE TWO GODS OF MY SOUL

I visited them this summer.

Courted one on a Dalmatian beach,
walked the hills of Herzegovina with the other.

O Herzegovina, forgotten sibling.
No one knows your name.

You gave me my tongue.
I give you American-chewed words.

## SPAGHETTI JUNCTION

Deep within the pocket of loneliness
lives a feeling whose name is pocket.

It tells me it's been energized lately.
It says, *When you find yourself*

*a citizen of two countries,*
*the third is never far.*

Then it pulls up a photograph
of Spaghetti Junction, a highway

interchange. As a teenager,
when Louisville first became

my town, I thought Spaghetti Junction
was a marketplace.

Pocket is waiting for me to admit
to this. In me a feeling of guilt

arises, though no one's stomach
slouched due to my ignorance.

## HWITTY REFUGEE

Murmur of waves.
The peeling guardrail paint

tickles cotton bottoms.
Borges made the licking

for licking eternity.
I make I for I:

from making tea to teasing cl-
ass. You know people

who pronounce *wittiest*
as if it had an h?

I'm their uncle.
Am Mr. Barnacle.

Lube me up with
lips, Johnny boy. Moy

country. Moy country.
Moy. I have three.

I collect in hope
of professor be.

I’m trifurcated, why
can’t my land?

What? says Father
of hearing hard.

A virgin of time, in time
will blossom.

Father daddy, come
to the park.

Swallow the question
mark.

## MOTHER, NEVER

Mother went inside
Mother, never
to emerge.

The summer was full
of fluff: pleasures
like kiwi fruit

waited for the pluck.
I cut the grass
for the first time.

With newsprint
Father made
the front yards

plump. Brother
ensured strangers'
stomachs did not

growl. At home,
we lurched
into each

other, feeding
food to the silence
in our midst.

## MEMORY LIVES

Memory lives
in a glass
jar.

I feed it to Mother
but Mother's teeth
are not real.

The local dentist
laughs.
"I don't do

implants.
No one trusts
them here."

Outside, roasted
chestnuts in mouths,
the town is waiting.

## THE CENTERS OF POWER

Thirty years old, a refugee,
in lush relation with morning
bowl of quinoa, a prim swimmer,
a connoisseur of nostalgia and regret,

impatient with the sweetness of the home-
grown onion, a cranky dresser,
a procurator of indecision.
Nothing fits: rained-on shoes, ripe Williams

pears, the sage blissing by a tree.
He's in a room with two windows and a Jack
Daniel's, a lent cocker spaniel purring.
In rooms with him dogs turn to cats.

For a long time he has wanted to be naked
but not one interlocutor speaks his language.
An applicant without a signature cannot
turn in an application.

A such applicant mouths, but not words.
The applicant lobbies for an increase
in the number of translation aids,
and a respective increase in insurance

plans that cover them.
He would like to live in the centers of power,
where phone babble moves mountains
and everyone goes out for lunch.

## THE PRACTICE

After fifteen years of preparation,
years long with sacrifice and effort,
he must face the reality:

there is nothing coming out of him.
The others don't know it yet.
In hushed awe they talk of things to come,

a golden time of flowering.
They resort to bees and honey
to make sense of the future.

But he knows.
The long years have been for nothing
but themselves.

## WHERE LOVE NAPS, THERE NIP I

There is only one dust in this world

All the hats, pens, and watches are made from it

The wrens sing of it, sing
in it

In it my ex-lover bathes

I am naked
today

and I was naked
last night

I ate a burnt-out cigarette and did not clean
my tongue

Most loving is fire: finite light

Feelings branch out

Feelings sing: Be you blithe
and bonny

Day starts with dawn, pink
or not

## PASTIME

Life is a tool without interest in fixing.
Monday and Tuesday whirl like eggs
in a well-oiled pan. On Sunday, a devotion
to fishing in snow-made lakes.

It's nice up there: domestic animals chase
chipmunks, horses enrich the soil, a peach packs
ecstasy in the mouth. I feel doubly
removed from belonging.

It feels good to appraise the natural world,
to think of the property appraiser who spent
most time in the bathroom, the smallest space
in the house. I liked him well enough. I too

poke life in situations of constraint and extract
the juices. Life is not a steak, nor is devotion
to breadth a sexy quality in a thinking creature,
yet this knowledge helps the way vinegar

applied to feet reduced childhood fevers.
Coyness is not a quality I aspire to, and there
is much to be said for subtle marinades.
But Sunday passes, the lakes freeze

and the roads grow hoary with snow.
The lights at home come on
before the birds have gone quiet.
I strip the trout of its armor.

## SOMEDAY I WILL LEARN

One day, I will say
goodbye to love as I
have lived it.

In the forest of the city,
chickadees will give themselves
to a two-tone call.

On the beach, I will let sand
touch me as if
for the first time:

we'll be friends.
Impressions of years
and years

crisscross, morphing
like the graying.
We leave pockets

of ourselves unlovable,
are afraid of mirrors.
We err and trademark.

***

## EXILE: A SUITE

### *Childhood Like Pepper*

The plum orchard
                    lives in childhood

I live alone

Three years no pleasure
                              but pleasure

          Green days
          Blue days

Pleasure over pleasure:
                              a finite onion

*The World With Evil Crackles*

Purr of plum          give me

Give stark medallions
slated for extinction

          (Father:
                    *Extinction is for broken hearts*)

The weaving must go on
if we are to wear clothes

Thusly we thicken

*Bosnia and Herzegovina*

The right solitude    lives in Bosnia
The wrong solitude    lives in Herzegovina

No—it's the other way around

*Whether You Love or Lever Power*

Nothing we own is on Mars nothing
at a desperate distance

Roses are flowers to be
looked at and this age
calls for chewing

My country wears silken clothes my country
is forward-thinking, knowing the countries' wont
to resemble the wind in time

First shrink, a new map, gristle
for geography

Nothing we own is on Mars

Then shrunk, a new name, the thrill
of start

Nothing at a desperate distance

All the while in the alleys all the while
across the boulevards the finite
pleasure barks at forever

Exit empire

## LOVE AND WAR

I am one born in Balkans son of a mother.
I was born the traditional way: a stork shook feathers;
out came I, in leathers.

My father was aghast.
My mother guessed his past.
My brother knew the candle wouldn't last.

I was given a gift six months of age—
a *musa paradisiaca*, yellow, with spots of beige.
I ate as much as I could, buried the rest in a cage.

At ten I met—oh lord—you.
You were a stratified lake.
I licked your epilimnion.

Your mother was a wild-haired politician.
Your father ran the hydroelectric dam.
Your siblings were your fans.

The school excursion took us to a kingdom by the sea.
I named you Anabel Li.
Anabel Li, I sang, Anabel Li: With you I want to be.

Then came the wind, then came the wave;
the cage grew big, I became its slave.
And you, Anabel Li, you ran away.

Now I ponder, and bananas grow.
I've moved away, yet life is slow.
It trickles, and trickling proclaims: I know.

## VAAG

I'm usually not preoccupied with pleasing adults.
There is something in me, a corner maybe,
that is afraid of grownups. I might have one
of those phobias. Without insurance it is hard
to get ahead because your head can't get checked.
My potential is a pond: in summer dry.
I read a lot. I watch TV too. I like my job.
I have been doing it for three years
and the boss tells me my kids are getting
into good high schools.
When I go to bed I imagine myself as a kid
shuffling off to private school.
This is not nostalgia. I know nostalgia.
Nostalgia is taking less and less time to appear.
I'm nostalgic for things I did last month.
At night I sigh about the morning. Do you think
that would be a good placard to bring to a rally
about health-insurance reform? I think it's too vague.
Once in high school I mispronounced vague.
Everybody looked at me strangely. They thought
I said fag. Chamberlain was vaag about Hitler.
I feel comfortable with you.

## HOME, I MISS HOME

Home, I miss
the other me,
the me who
misses the
now me.

## CANNOT NOT

If you were, what would you?
Soft library morning light, a breeze
in wintertime? The street fullness that comes
with marching beings?

I'm sure of one thing—I cannot not
check my rank. I tell myself it is a very being
thing to do, do not worry, it is okay.
One glance is enough to topple the day.

Normally, in the afternoon, the afternoon and I
mend socks while playing with our locks.
A calm, relaxing activity. We say, to whoever
might be listening, let it come.

The conversations with the beach, too,
are euphonious. It knows me better
than my mother. She lives in the town
of poplars and mumbles through her days.

I speak to her on the phone, *This is your son*,
and she asks, *Where is he?* Well, now not even
that much of a response. She used to like
ficuses. My family doesn't boast many plant

lovers, with males usually caring less
than females. I am the exception,
but only in certain climates. Close to the sea,
my soul desires green.

Now the snow is my companion, keeping
guard at the door, daring the unknown to knock
on its cold crystals, snug as snails. I watch
from the warmth, laughing at the me of me.

## BREATHWORK

Between my transformation and yours
lives oxidized breathwork.
I am waiting to be a waiting, a grape's
patient globe at fall's expiring.

Occult spices cannot save the onion.
The union.
At a younger age I would have apologized
and bracketed the mistake.

Tuesday nights in the Baptist Church basement,
Chinese women gather to play mahjong.
They are polite and fierce at once.
I wish I were the silk woven into their blouses.

All these years, and the desire for community
still paces my halls.
*Du musst dein Leben ändern* is one thing
we never stop telling ourselves.

If I were a bright red ball, what kind of ball would I be?

## SUMMERTIME IN DALMATIA

Two women drink midday beer and complain about the lack of vanilla
ice cream cones at the corner store.

The smell of fried fish and olive-drizzled chard nips the noses of soccer-
enchanted kids.

An old man tames a pipe, two shirtless men play chess,
five handle the cards with tongue-licked fingers.

Like sporadic protocols of lazy nations, seagulls patrol the skies and
determine the quota of the day's catch.

A woman puts a crate of freshly picked figs on a sun-inflamed bench to dry.
Her husband goes trash bin to trash bin in search of plastic and cans.

The grown son trims his toenails under a tamarind tree.

The man fond of his bicycle buys groceries, tells the lady at the checkout:
*I don't understand life, I got married late.*

Fires ravage Turkey and fire-fighting aircraft are sent to help.
The locals are proud.

It is Saturday, the wedding day. The guests go to the groom's, then the bride's,
then the church, then the reception hall. The minimum gift is one hundred
euros.

Tourists stalk the promenade, taking pictures of a blue 1984 Renault 4.

The pizzeria on the south side of town has new, oil-resistant tablecloths. It employs two waiters and one waitress.

The post office is closed.

## CAMPING TRIP

The needle has lost its compass,
Brother has seen the bear,
Father is turning back.
*But the tent is new!*

Mother says.
*I want to use it.*
The look she throws Father
is a beggar's look only at first.

We camp three nights.
I save ants from frozen morning
ground, Brother kills them
leading up to lunch.

Father pulls out yin and yang,
Mother sends him to a field of manure.
*You and your Eastern philosophizing*, she says
and cooks beans to upset father's stomach.

I laugh uneasily: beans don't agree with me.
But I'm young and it's too early to admit
to a failing like that—a Balkan child
unable to digest beans.

Under an oak Brother pins me,
hovers above me.
Spit hangs from his mouth.
It grows thin and long as it moves

to kiss me.
*I'm not afraid of you, ant killer!*
Mother leaves the tent at midnight,
clearing the air in front of her.

Father dreams.
Brother snores.
I count the stars that glue themselves
to the nylon roof.

## LETTER TO A VACUUM

Four limbs puncture the earth.
Turn me on my back, turn me innocuous.
Show me celestial barricades;
tell me I can walk only in circles.
Tell me you are a biting
to which I must return.

Turn me into cyan.
No, turn me into a word.
Utter me blank—say blank
and point to me. Then think: he is a word.

Play me.
Touch.
Assume my hands.
Glue my tongue on top of yours and say:
My words are your dusk.
Be rough, make me knit you hats.

Plant bugs
in my fingers;
watch me ride
vacuum-cities.

Manifest me. Molest me. Mother me.
Atrociously father me.

## ETERNAL MONDAY

Months pass and I don't feel
twinges of jealousy toward those
who got there first with the great
idea. This happens when I'm not
reading much. Other times, delight
and deflation. Wouldn't that be
a nice first line: "Delight and deflation
come at the same time." I wonder
if it has already been exploited. I could search
with quotation marks. Or I could tell myself,
Don't worry, go ahead and make it yours.
When we make something ours, the world
gets smaller. Pleasure, after all, buds
most abundantly in fenced gardens.
In youth I ran around lovers, lovers
who loved me, but never felt cemented
by love. It was a case of the eternal Monday:
time to kiss was time to go to work,
and the timing couldn't have been worse—
the beginning of the labor week. Still,
labor I did. War made me learn
a new language. Hooked, I learned another.
In my pocket passports proliferated.
You could say alliteration no longer
pleases the way it once did, and that the latinate
*proliferated* grates. I myself have made similar
arguments. Interestingly, the upshot of thinking

self-consciously is feeling like a machine.
It is hard not to return to looking up as a way
to settle wondering. Of course, metaphor aside,
we don't do much looking up. If we did,
we would know it's the clouds that are fickle,
not the sun. That seems like a good stopping point,
yet it gives off a whiff of—smugness?
I cannot help what I feel any more than the sun
can help being there. I cannot help
being in love with Ruefle's milkshake
and Koethe's swimmer. It is risky to name poems
in a poem, yet if I failed to name, I wouldn't be writing
in this moment, on this day, watching yellow
daffodils in the wind sway. And if I failed
to discover my clouds, the clouds
that don't let me see my life as it really is,
I also failed to imperil the machinery.
Hurrah for the rain.

## SURFACES

I want to make love
with a ruin

Scrub the surface, slide fingers across
the wave-infested top

Tickle stone, tickle stone:
I am made of flesh and bone

Paper lives longer

And Father on mind?

And my father on my mind

Father: you were a plum-keeper

The experience passes,
a swallow knighting the dawn

## ACTION AT A DISTANCE

Greet the summers of childhood and stone.
Greet the the's the a's the an's the tongue
sifted through and outspit.

I went to sheets with a new language
and my old country sighed.
In it I had discovered the lonely thrill, much too inadequate

for a body that hairs.
Hirsute me surfaced in Kentucky.
Whoever speaks of satisfactory humpty-dumpty within frenzy of

nationalism is a fool.
I left the sea.
Before I left the sea, I left the mountains.

For my country contains twain: place of birth
and place of bath.
Blessed small me, Tito's pioneer, poking holes

in Herzegovina's valleys and dales, adding to the volume
of the Adriatic.
Adriatic: like a sibling. For twenty years I've failed to adjust

to Morton salt.
I carried in my left pocket the tears the country
packed. Tried to cry my own but Brandon and Kelly and Beverly

Hills occupied the rest. I couldn't help it, country.
You were something of a scandal.
Do you miss me as much as I think

about you? The jigs of history made you younger
than me. You pluck me dry of wise, feed me
breath of cigarettes, sludge coffee, lambs.

Where lie the days when you and I were one,
when letters united the scout with his notional womb?
Passed is passed, but the passing lasts.

# THE UNDERGROUND

Those under us are not dead.
They are dancers. We are the music.

Before I knew, I wanted to go down in ashes—
down the river Neretva.

Now I want to be buried.
It doesn't matter where.

Five major highways span the underground.
They are, they say, superbly connected.

## *ACKNOWLEDGMENTS*

Many thanks to the editors and staff of the publications in which these poems first appeared, sometimes in earlier versions:

*AGNI:* "Action at a Distance"; *Believer Online*: "Twice There Was a Country"; *Better Magazine*: "QueerRefugeeCatholicMuslim" (as "Again the Fable Dies"); *Country Music*: "Surfaces"; *Crazyhorse*: "The Old Bridge in Mostar," "In a Photograph Your Hands Melt"; *DIAGRAM*: "The Body"; *Fence*: "Vaag," "Good Luck," "Ashbery in Bosnia"; *Forklift, Ohio*: "Camping Trip," "Where Love Naps, There Nip I"; *Harpur Palate*: "Letter to a Vacuum"; *Iowa Review*: "Spaghetti Junction"; *Missouri Review Online*: "Little by Little"; *Narrative*: "The Underground," "Auntie Oracle," "The Practice"; *Phantom Limb*: "Primer Ruffled by Wind"; *Prairie Schooner*: "Breathwork," "The Age of Monkeys," "Cannot Not"; *smoking glue gun*: "Dear Universe," "Love and War"; *Southern Review*: "Double Negative"

This book was made possible with generous support from the Michener Center for Writers at the University of Texas at Austin, the Fine Arts Work Center in Provincetown, and the University of Utah.

Enormous gratitude to everyone at the Cleveland State University Poetry Center, especially Caryl Pagel and Hilary Plum. And endless thanks to Brenda Hillman for selecting the book.

Thank you to my high school English teachers, Cathy "Bubara" Green and Ms. Thompson, for their love of grammar and literature, and for encouraging me to write creatively.

A special thank you to Kyle Coma-Thompson. You helped me step back into the poetic journey.

To Fedja Buric—my rock, my shrink, my Bosnian pie. What would I do without your friendship? In this refugee existence, you're my refuge.

For their kindness, support and encouragement, I'm grateful to my friends and teachers: Jackie Balderrama, Jessica Rae Bergamino, Jericho Brown, Will Clark, Kate Coles, Lidija Dimkovska, Noam Dorr, JP Grasser, Linda Gregg, Matt Hart, Laurel Hunt, John James, Douglas Kearney, Brigit Pegeen Kelly, Taisia Kitaiskaia, Elizabeth Kuhn, Michael McGriff, John Michael, Corey Miller, Maggie Nelson, Naomi Shihab Nye, Lisa Olstein, Jackie Osherow, Allison Pauly, Paisley Rekdal, Sarah-Jane Ripa, Josh Rivkin, Tom Sleigh, Claire Sylvester Smith, Brian Weinberg, Monica Wheelock, Cori Winrock, Dean Young, and Javier Zamora.

Finally, thank you to my family for love and support. And to my mother, Ljerka—I miss you beyond words.

**RECENT CLEVELAND STATE UNIVERSITY POETRY CENTER PUBLICATIONS**

*Editors: Caryl Pagel & Hilary Plum*

**Poetry**

*World'd Too Much: The Selected Poetry of Russell Atkins* ed. Kevin Prufer and Robert E. McDonough
*Advantages of Being Evergreen* by Oliver Baez Bendorf
*My Fault* by Leora Fridman
*Orient* by Nicholas Gulig
*Age of Glass* by Anna Maria Hong
*In One Form to Find Another* by Jane Lewty
*50 Water Dreams* by Siwar Masannat
*daughterrarium* by Sheila McMullin
*The Bees Make Money in the Lion* by Lo Kwa Mei-en
*Residuum* by Martin Rock
*Festival* by Broc Rossell
*Sun Cycle* by Anne Lesley Selcer
*Bottle the Bottles the Bottles the Bottles* by Lee Upton

**Essays**

*I Liked You Better Before I Knew You So* Well by James Allen Hall
*A Bestiary* by Lily Hoang
*Codependence* by Amy Long
*The Leftovers* by Shaelyn Smith

**Translations**

*Scorpionic Sun* by Mohammed Khaïr-Eddine, translated by Conor Bracken
*I Burned at the Feast: Selected Poems of Arseny Tarkovsky* translated by Philip Metres and Dimitri Psurtsev

For a complete list of titles visit www.csupoetrycenter.com